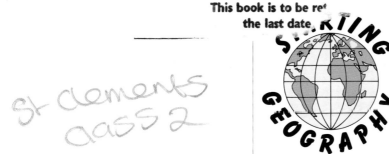

St clements
class 2

Houses and Homes

Written by
Helen Barden

Illustrated by
Robert Wheeler

Wayland

Books in the series

Clothes and Costumes   Landscapes
Conservation   Resources
Houses and Homes   Water
Journeys   Weather and Climate

This edition published in 1994 by
Wayland (Publishers) Ltd

First published in 1992 by
Wayland (Publishers) Ltd
61 Western Road, Hove
East Sussex, BN3 1JD, England

Series editor: Mandy Suhr
Designer: Jean Wheeler
Consultants: Julie Warne and Lorraine Harrison

British Library Cataloguing in Publication Data

Barden, Helen
Houses and Homes.–(Starting geography)
I. Title   II. Series
728.3

HARDBACK ISBN 0-7502-0331-5

PAPERBACK ISBN 0-7502-0611-X

Typeset by DP Press, Sevenoaks, Kent
Printed in Italy by Rotolito Lombarda, S.p.A., Milan

Contents

The words in **bold** are explained in the glossary.

What is a home?

Everyone needs a home. A home is a place that gives shelter and protection.

It is a place where you live, eat and sleep.

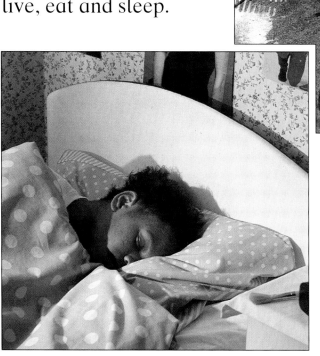

There are many kinds of houses. They are different because many are built to suit the way of life of the people that live in them. The weather and the landscape also affect the way houses are built and designed.

Some houses are built with bricks and **tiles**.

Others may be built with wood, or sticks and grass.

Some houses are built so that they float on water.

 **Activity**

What is your home like? Can you make a model of a house?

Where do you live?

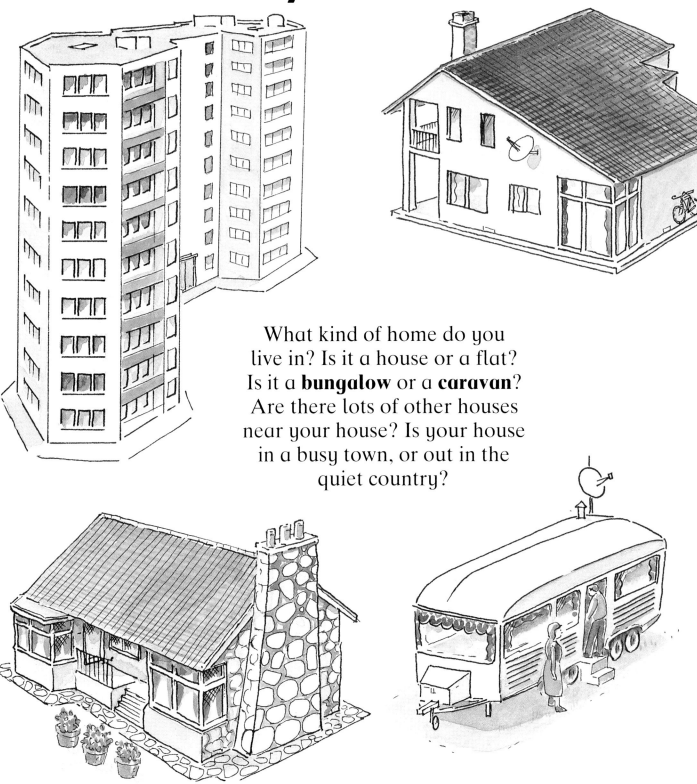

What kind of home do you
live in? Is it a house or a flat?
Is it a **bungalow** or a **caravan**?
Are there lots of other houses
near your house? Is your house
in a busy town, or out in the
quiet country?

What other buildings are near to your house?
Are you near a park … or shops …

or a railway station?

Can you describe the place where you live?

Activity

Draw a map to show
your house and street
and the buildings that
are nearby. What other
things can you think of
to mark on your map?

What do we need?

Wherever people choose to live they need to be near food and water. Often they choose to live together in a group.

This is called a **settlement**. As a settlement grows and more people come to live there, many things are needed.

Hospitals and schools need to be built.

Shops and markets are needed for people to buy food, clothing and other things.

People need places to meet and play together, like cinemas, parks and swimming pools.

Roads and railways are built so that we can travel and move goods around the country.

Big places and small places

People often choose to live in a place because they can work there. In large settlements, like towns and cities, there are factories and shops and many other places that provide jobs for people.

Millions of people live in Delhi, in India. ▼

Some settlements are very small. They do not have many people living in them, like this one near Mount Everest in Nepal.

A settlement may be small because the land is very **mountainous**, or very dry, so it is difficult to build houses and live there.
Sometimes it is small because the land is needed for farming. This is a small farming **community** in the USA.▶

Building a house

The way a house is built depends on many things. Many people build their houses with **materials** they can find easily, like wood.

Grass and straw have been used for building for many years. They can be used to make a warm and dry roof for a home.

This house has been built with wooden logs from the trees nearby.

Today, many houses all over the world are built with bricks or **concrete**. These are held together with **cement** which dries as hard as rock.▶

What is your house built of?

13

Homes in cold places

The weather can affect the way in which people's houses are designed and built. Houses in cold, snowy countries must give lots of shelter against the cold **temperatures** and icy winds. They need thick walls with **insulation** to keep heat in.

Timber is often used to build houses in the cold countries of northern Scandinavia. These houses need less heat to warm them up than those built of stone or brick.

In places where a lot of rain or snow falls, houses may have long, sloping roofs so that water can run off easily.▲

Heating is very important in cold places. Electricity may be used to heat **radiators** and electric fires. Other houses may be heated by burning **fuels** such as coal, wood or oil.▶

Homes in hot places

In hot, sunny countries, houses have to provide shade from the heat of the sun. Many houses are painted white.

The white colour on the outside of the walls reflects the heat of the sun and keeps the inside cool. This house is in Greece.

Houses in hot places often have blinds or **window shutters** to keep out the sun during the hottest parts of the day.

Some houses have flat roofs that can be used as another room. Some homes may have an **air-conditioning system**.

Activity

Imagine you are living somewhere very hot with lots of rain. Design a house that you think would be suitable.

Rich and Poor

Within most countries, the homes that people live in can be very different. Homes in cities will be different to homes that are in the countryside.

The homes may also be different because of the amount of money that people have. Many people cannot choose the sort of home that they would like to live in because they do not have enough money.

These pictures show a city in Brazil where many very rich people live in large, expensive houses. The poor people live in very different kinds of houses around the edge of the city.▼

Some people do not have homes at all. They may have to live on the streets because they are so poor. This girl is homeless. She lives on the streets of London, in Britain. Do you think this is fair?

Close together, far apart

As towns grow, they can become overcrowded with people. Sometimes they are so crowded that there is no more space for building houses.

Houses may have to be built closer together, or built on top of each other, like these flats in China.▲

Some people choose to live in places far away from other people and houses. A **lighthouse-keeper** has to live far away from his friends because of his job.▶

This sheep farm is in Australia. The farmer has many people working for him, but his nearest neighbour is many kilometres away. He goes to town by plane and stays overnight, because it takes so long to get there.

Moving home

Have you ever moved house? It can be very exciting to move.

Sometimes people move for a new job or because a bigger house is needed for a new baby.

Sometimes people move to live near their friends and family.

Sometimes it is because some of the family have moved away and a smaller house would be better.

Activity

Imagine you are moving. Design a poster that advertises your house for sale. Make sure you put in all the good things about your house as well as the size and where it is.

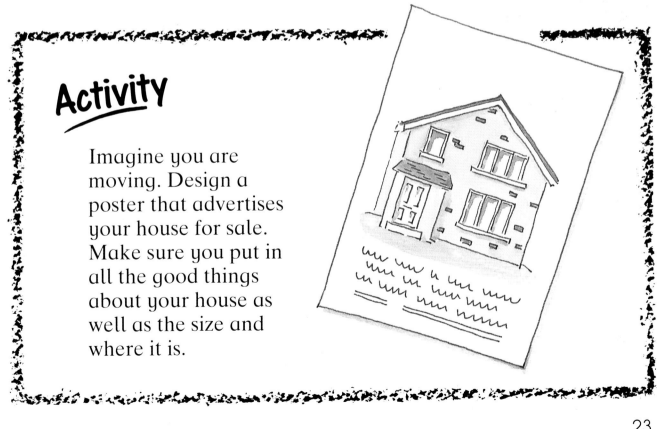

On the move

Some people move all the time. These people in Britain are **travellers**. They live in caravans and move around the country.▶

These people also move around. Their homes are made to make moving easy. They live in tents so that they can move and set up home very quickly. ▼

▲Sadly, these Kurdish people have had to move because their houses have been destroyed by war. They may have to move far away from their old home to find safety.

People live where they can get food and water for themselves and water for their crops and animals. In some countries, if the rain does not come and there is a **drought**, families may have to move to stay alive. ▶

A town then and now

Towns are growing and changing all the time. Some towns have grown very quickly. Where there used to be fields and open spaces there are now **housing estates**, shops, factories and roads. They all provide for the new people who have moved into the town.

This old postcard shows a small town near the sea in Britain. Seventy years ago it looked like this. Now it is very different.

This photograph shows the same place today. Can you see how it has changed and grown?

What can you see that is different in this photograph?

Activity

What can you find out about the place where you live? How do you think it may have looked in the past?

My ideal house

This is how some people think houses will look in the future.

Have you ever seen houses like these? They are very unusual.

This **astronaut** is living in space. Maybe one day lots of other people will live there too. What do you think?

Activity

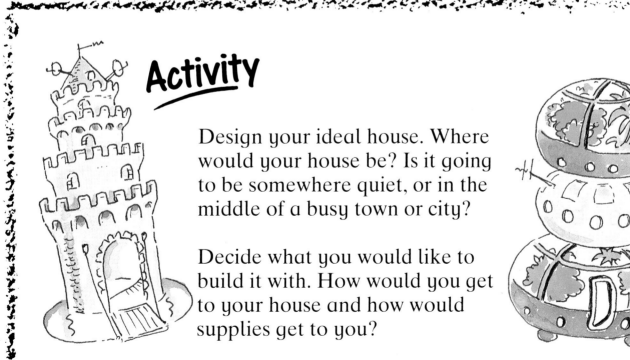

Design your ideal house. Where would your house be? Is it going to be somewhere quiet, or in the middle of a busy town or city?

Decide what you would like to build it with. How would you get to your house and how would supplies get to you?

Glossary

Air-conditioning system   A system of machines that move and cool the air inside a car or building.

Astronaut   A person trained to travel in space.

Bungalow   A house built on only one level.

Caravan   A home on wheels that can be moved from place to place.

Cement   A grey powder made by burning chalk, limestone and clay in a kiln. When it is mixed with water it dries as hard as rock. It is used to hold bricks together.

Community   A group of people living together.

Concrete   A building material made from mixing cement with sand and stones.

Drought   A long period of dry weather, creating a shortage of water.

Fuels   Materials that can be burned to give heat or power.

Housing estate   A large area of land covered by houses.

Insulation   Extra layers added to walls to stop heat from escaping from inside a house.

Lighthouse-keeper   A person who looks after a lighthouse.

Materials   Things needed for making something. Natural materials come from the land. Other materials may be made by people using machines.

Mountainous   An area of mountains.

Radiators   Room heaters made from pipes that hot water passes through.

Settlement   A group of people living together.

Temperature   How hot or cold something is.

Tiles   Flat thin slabs of clay or rubber used to cover roofs.

Timber   Wood when it is used as a building material.

Travellers   A group of people living all over Europe who do not live in one place but travel around.

Window shutters   Movable covers for the outside of a window.

Finding out more

Books to read

Houses and Homes by Carolyn Crooke (MacDonald)

Homes in Cold Places by Alan James (Wayland, 1987)

Homes in Hot Places by Alan James (Wayland, 1987)

Houses and Homes by Heinz Kurt (World's Work)

Houses and Homes by Theodore Rowland-Entwistle (Wayland, 1987)

The House by Carol Watson (Usborne, 1980)

Picture acknowlegements

The photographs in this book were supplied by: Cephas 24 below, Bruce Coleman Ltd 4 above, 5 above left, 12 above and below, 14, 21, 25 below, East Sussex Libraries 26; Eye Ubiquitous 15, 5 below, 7 above right, 27; Jimmy Holmes 5 below, 7 above right; David Hoffman 19; Hutchison 18 below and above; LINK 7 below, 16, 17 right, 25 above; PHOTRI 9 right, 12 above left; TOPHAM 29. Tony Stone Worldwide 11 above, 28 above and below; Tim Woodcock 4 below, 7 above left, 13; Zefa 5 above, 8, 9 left, 10, 11, below, 17 left, 20 below, 23.

Index